CONTENTS

SOFT FLORALS

BOLD PATTERNS

LIGHT AND LACY

COOL CLASSICS

WARM AND COZY

BRIGHT AND FUN

For pattern inquiries, please visit www.knitsimplemag.com or www.go-crafty.com

FINISHED MEASUREMENTS

Approx 6½"/16.5cm wide x 65"/165cm long (excluding flowers and leaves)

GAUGE

17 sts to 5"/12.5cm and 9 rows to 4"/10cm over dc using size J/10 (6mm) crochet hook.
Take time to check gauge.

NOTES

1 Scarf is worked lengthwise.
2 When changing colors, draw new color through last 2 lps on hook, then ch and turn.

STITCH GLOSSARY

tr5tog [Yo twice, insert hook into next st and draw up lp, (yo, draw through 2 lps on hook) twice] 5 times, yo and draw through all 6 lps on hook.
dc2tog [Yo, insert hook into next st and draw up lp, yo, draw through 2 lps on hook] twice, yo and draw through all 3 lps on hook.
dc3tog [Yo, insert hook into next st and draw up lp, yo, draw through 2 lps on hook] 3 times, yo and draw through all 4 lps on hook.

SCARF

With A, ch 223.
Row 1 Dc in 4th ch from hook and in ch across, changing to B—220 sts. Ch 3, turn.
Row 2 Dc in each st across, changing to C. Ch 3, turn.
Rep row 2 for pat st and work stripe pat as foll: 1 row each in C, D, E, F, G, A, B, C, D, E, F, G. Fasten off.

FLOWERS (make 10 pieces)
Center
With A, ch 7. Join ch with a sl st forming a ring.
Rnd 1 (RS) Ch 3 (counts as 1 dc), work 4 dc in ring, [ch 2, work 5 dc in ring] 4 times, ch 2, join rnd with a sl st in 3rd ch of beg ch-3—5 ch-2 sps. Fasten off.

PETALS
With RS facing, join G with a sl st in any ch-2 sp.
Rnd 2 [Ch 6, tr5tog, ch 6, sl st in next ch-sp] 5 times—5 petals. Fasten off. Make 1 more flower using A for center and G for petals.

Make 2 more flowers each using E for center and A for petals, D for center and B for petals, B for center and C for petals, and D for center and A for petals.

LEAVES (make 14 pieces)
With F, ch 3.
Row 1 Work 3 dc in 3rd ch from hook. Ch 2, turn.
Row 2 Work 2 dc in first st, dc in next st, work 2 dc in last st—5 dc. Ch 2, turn.
Row 3 Work 2 dc in first st, dc in next 3 sts, work 2 dc in last st—7 dc. Ch 2, turn.
Row 4 Dc in each st across. Ch 2, turn.
Row 5 Dc2tog, dc in next 3 sts, dc2tog—5 dc. Ch 2, turn.
Row 6 Dc2tog, dc in next st, dc2tog—3 dc. Ch 2, turn.
Row 7 Dc3tog. Fasten off. Make 7 more leaves using F and 6 more using D.

FINISHING

Block scarf lightly to measurements. Referring to photo, arrange 5 flowers and 7 leaves on each end of scarf. Sew pieces in place using yarn colors to match.

TOOLKIT

YARN

- (4) *Vanna's Choice* by Lion Brand Yarn Co., 3½oz/100g, 170yd/156m acrylic in wild berry (A), dusty blue (B), rose (C), beige (D), dusty purple (E), dusty green (F), and dusty rose (G)

HOOK

- Size J/10 (6mm) crochet hook *or size to obtain gauge*

MARINE FLAIR

Jack Deutsch

■ ■ ■ ■

FINISHED MEASUREMENTS
Approx 7"/17.5cm wide x 56"/142cm long

GAUGE
9 dc and ch-2 sps, and 9 rows to 4"/10cm over mesh pat st using size C/2 (2.75mm) crochet hook.
Take time to check gauge.

SCARF
Ch 53.
Row 1 Dc in 8th ch from hook (counts as ch 2, sk 2 ch and 1 dc), *ch 2, sk next 2 ch, dc in next ch; rep from * to end—16 ch-2 sps. Turn.
Row 2 Ch 5 (counts as 1 dc and ch 2), sk first 2 ch, *dc in next dc, ch 2; rep from *, end sk last 2 ch, dc in 3rd ch of t-ch of row below. Turn. Rep row 2 for mesh pat st until piece measures 56"/142cm from beg. Fasten off.

FINISHING
Block scarf lightly to measurements.

TOOLKIT

YARN
- (1) 3½oz/100g, 440yd/410m of any fingering weight variegated mohair blend

HOOK
- Size C/2 (2.75mm) crochet hook or *size to obtain gauge*

STRIPED LACE SCARF

TOOLKIT

YARN
- (5) 5¼oz/150g, 410yd/375m of any bulky weight wool blend

HOOK
- Size I/9 (5.5mm) crochet hook or *size to obtain gauge*

■ ■ ■ ■

FINISHED MEASUREMENTS
Approx 8"/20cm wide x 64"/162.5cm long (excluding fringe)

GAUGE
14 sts and 6 rows to 4"/10cm over shell st pat using size I/9 (5.5mm) crochet hook.
Take time to check gauge.

SCARF
Ch 31. **Row 1** Work 4 dc in 4th ch from hook, sk next 4 ch, hdc in next ch, *ch 2, sk next ch, dc in next ch, ch 1, sk next ch, dc in next ch, ch 1, sk next ch, work 5 dc in next ch (shell made), sk next 4 ch, hdc in next ch; rep from * once more. Ch 3, turn. **Row 2** Work 4 dc in first hdc, hdc in 5th dc of first shell, *ch 2, dc in next dc, ch 1, dc in next dc, ch 1, work 5 dc in next hdc, hdc in 5th dc of next shell; rep from

* once more, ending rep with hdc in 3rd ch of ch-3 t-ch of last shell. Ch 3, turn. Rep row 2 for shell st pat until piece measures 64"/162.5cm from beg. Fasten off.

FINISHING
Block scarf lightly to measurements.

FRINGE
Cut 14"/33cm strands of yarn. Using 4 strands for each fringe, attach 13 fringes evenly spaced across each end of scarf. Trim ends evenly.

Jack Deutsch

Jack Deutsch

TOOLKIT

YARN
- (4) *Simply Soft Solids* by Caron, 6oz/170g, 330yd/302m acrylic in black (A) and off-white (B)

HOOK
- Size J/10 (6mm) crochet hook or *size to obtain gauge*

FINISHED MEASUREMENTS
Approx 7½"/19cm wide x 59"/150cm long

GAUGE
13 sts and 16 rows to 4"/10cm over pat st using size J/10 (6mm) crochet hook.
Take time to check gauge.

NOTES
1 When changing colors, draw new color through last 2 lps on hook.
2 Carry color not in use along side edge of work.

STITCH GLOSSARY
Long double crochet (Ldc) Yo, insert hook from front to back in st indicated, yo and draw up a long lp, [yo and draw through 2 lps on hook] twice.

SCARF
With A, ch 26.

Row 1 Sc in 2nd ch from hook and in each ch across, changing to B in last st—25 sts. Ch 1, turn.
Row 2 Sc in each st across. Ch 1, turn
Row 3 Rep row 2, changing to A in last st. Ch 1, turn.
Row 4 Sc in first st, Ldc in 3rd sc of 3 rows below, *sc in next st on working row, Ldc in 2nd st from previous Ldc 3 rows below, sc in next st on working row, Ldc in same st as previous Ldc, sc in next st on working row, Ldc in 2nd st from previous Ldc 3 rows below, sc in next st on working row, Ldc in 4th st from previous Ldc 3 rows below; rep from * once more, end sc in next st on working row, Ldc in 2nd st from previous Ldc 3 rows below, sc in next st on working row, Ldc in same st as previous Ldc, sc in next st on working row, Ldc in 2nd st from previous Ldc 3 rows below, sc in last st on working row. Ch 1, turn.
Row 5 Sc in each sc across, changing to B in last st. Ch 1, turn.
Row 6 Rep row 4.
Row 7 Rep row 5, changing to A in last st. Ch 1, turn. Rep rows 4 to 7 for pat st and stripe pat until piece measures 59"/150cm from beg, end with row 4. Fasten off.

FINISHING
Block scarf lightly to measurements.

PETAL POWER

Jack Deutsch

TOOLKIT

YARN

- **3** 5¼oz/150g, 360yd/330m of any DK weight cotton in red (A)

- 8¾oz/250g, 600yd/550m in orange (B) and burgundy (C)

HOOK

- Size G/6 (4mm) crochet hook *or size to obtain gauge*

FINISHED MEASUREMENTS

Approx 3½"/9cm wide x 76"/193cm long

GAUGE

22 sts to 4"/10cm and 3 rows to 2½"/6.5cm over ruffle pat using size G/6 (4mm) crochet hook.
Take time to check gauge.

STITCH GLOSSARY

Double treble crochet (dtr) Yo 3 times, insert hook into st, yo and draw up a lp, [yo and draw through 2 lps on hook] 4 times.

SCARF

With A, crochet a 70"/178cm long ch.
Row 1 (RS) Dtr in 5th ch from hook, work 4 dtr in same ch, *work 5 dtr in next ch; rep from * across. Fasten off.
Row 2 With RS facing, join B with a sl st in first st, ch 3, work 2 tr in same st as joining, *work 3 tr in next st; rep from * across. Fasten off.
Row 3 With RS facing, join C with a sl st in first st, ch 1, hdc in same st as joining, *work 2 hdc in next st; rep from * across. Fasten off.

TOOLKIT

YARN
- 🔵③ 7oz/200g, 480yd/440m of any DK weight wool

HOOK
- Size H/8 (5mm) afghan hook or *size to obtain gauge*

Jack Deutsch

FINISHED MEASUREMENTS
Approx 7"/17.5cm wide x 45"/114.5cm long (excluding fringe)

GAUGE
20 sts and 14 rows to 4"/10cm over tunisian (afghan) st using size H/8 (5mm) afghan hook.
Take time to check gauge.

NOTE
Each row of tunisian (afghan) st is worked in two halves. The first half is worked from right to left and the second half is worked from left to right.

SCARF
Ch 35.
Row 1 (first half) Retaining all lps on hook, insert hook into 2nd ch from hook, yo and draw up a lp, *insert hook into next ch, yo and draw up a lp; rep from * across—35 lps on hook.
Row 1 (second half) Yo, draw through first lp on hook, *yo and draw through next 2 lps on hook; rep from * until 1 lp rem on hook.
Row 2 (first half) Retaining all lps on hook, insert hook under 2nd vertical thread from side edge of the previous row, yo and draw up a lp, *insert hook under next vertical thread, yo and draw up a lp; rep from * across. Turn.

Row 2 (second half) Yo, draw through first lp on hook, *yo and draw through next 2 lps on hook; rep from * until 1 lp rem on hook. Rep row 2 for tunisian (afghan) st until piece measures 45"/ 114.5cm from beg.
Last row Insert hook under 2nd vertical thread from side edge of the previous row, yo and draw up a lp, yo and draw through both lps on hook, *insert hook under next vertical thread, yo and draw up a lp, yo and draw through both lps on hook; rep from * across. Fasten off.

FINISHING
Block scarf lightly to measurements.

FRINGE
Cut 15"/38cm strands of yarn. Using 3 strands for each fringe, attach 17 fringes evenly spaced across each end of scarf. Trim ends evenly.

Quenet

FINISHED MEASUREMENTS
Approx 5"/12.5cm wide x 67"/170cm long

GAUGE
One 7-dc scallop to 2"/5cm and 4 rows scallop st to 3"/7.5cm over scallop pat st using size K/10½ (7mm) hook.
Take time to check gauge.

STITCH GLOSSARY
CL (cluster) Work (yo, insert hook into st, yo, draw loop through st, yo, draw through 2 loops) over the number of sts indicated, yo, draw through all loops on hook.

SCALLOP STITCH PATTERN
Ch a multiple of 10 plus 6 ch plus 1 extra for base ch.

Row 1 Work 1 sc in 2nd ch from hook, 1 sc in next ch, *skip 3 ch, 7 dc in next ch, skip 3 ch, 1 sc in each of next 3 ch; rep from * to last 4 ch, skip 3 ch, 4 dc in last ch. Ch 1, turn.

Row 2 Work 1 sc in each of first 2 sts, *ch 3, 1 CL over next 7 sts, ch 3, 1 sc in each of next 3 sts; rep from * to last 4 sts, ch 3, 1 CL over last 4 sts, skip t-ch. Ch 3, turn.

Row 3 Counting ch 3 as 1 dc, work 3 dc into first st, *skip ch-3 sp, 1 sc in each of next 3 sc, skip ch-3 sp, 7 dc into the loop that closed next CL; rep from *, end with skip ch-3 sp, 1 sc in each of last 2 sc, skip t-ch. Ch 3, turn.

Row 4 Counting ch 3 as 1 dc, skip first st, 1 CL over next 3 sts, *ch 3, 1 sc in each of next 3 sts, ch 3, 1 CL over next 7 sts; rep from *, end with ch 3, 1 sc in next st, 1 sc in top of t-ch.

Ch 1, turn.

Row 5 Work 1 sc in each of first 2 sc, *skip ch-3 sp, 7 dc into the loop that closed next CL, skip ch-3 sp, 1 sc in each of next 3 sc; rep from *, end skip ch-3 sp, 4 dc in top of t-ch. Ch 1, turn.

Rep rows 2-5 for scallop stitch pattern.

SCARF
With A, ch 217. Work row 1 of scallop st pat. Change to B and work rows 2 and 3 of scallop st pat. Change to A and work rows 4 and 5 of scallop st pat. Fasten off.
Return to opposite side of scarf (base ch edge) and join A, beg at the end with 2 sc. With A, work row 5 of scallop st pat, working 7 dc into same ch-sp as 7 dc scallop of row 1. Change to B and work rows 2 and 3 of scallop st pat. Fasten off.

TOOLKIT

YARN
- 🌀6 7oz/200g, 200yd/180m of any super-bulky wool blend in red (A)

- 5¼oz/150g, 150yd/135m in coral (B)

HOOK
- Size K/10½ (7mm) crochet hook or *size to obtain gauge*

Quenet

TOOLKIT

YARN
- (1) 3½oz/100g, 380yd/350m of any fingering weight wool in charcoal (A) and grey (B)

HOOK
- Size C/2 (2.5mm) crochet hook or *size to obtain gauge*

FINISHED MEASUREMENTS
7"/18cm wide x 54"/137cm long, excluding fringe

GAUGE
20 dc and 9 dc rows to 4"/10cm over dc pat st foll chart using size C/2 (2.5mm) hook.
Take time to check gauge.

NOTES
1 When changing colors foll chart, work dc with chart designated color until only 2 loops rem on hook, draw the next color through these 2 loops on hook.
2 Work over color not in use so that color is carried along at top of last dc row while working.
3 When working chart rows 5-8, after completing last dc, ch 2 with same color first worked, then ch 1 with new color.

SCARF
With A, ch 37.
Row 1 (RS) Work 1 dc in 4th ch from hook, 1 dc in each of next 4 ch, 1 dc in next ch *drawing B through last 2 lps on hook, [work 1 dc with B drawing A through last 2 lps on hook, work 1 dc with A drawing B through last 2 lps on hook] 3 times, work 1 dc with B drawing A through last 2 loops on hook, work 1 dc in each of next 7 ch with A; rep from * once more. Ch 3, turn. This is the first row of the chart with the ch-3 at beg of row counting as 1 dc. Beg with row 2 of chart, cont to foll chart as set up, rep rows 1-8 a total of 14 times. Then, rep rows 1-4 once. Fasten off.

FINISHING
Block lightly, if necessary.

FRINGE
Cut each fringe 6"/15cm long (36 lengths of A and 32 lengths of B) using 2 lengths for each individual fringe and working 3 A fringe along each block in A and 4 B fringe to match each B stripe in 2-color block, attach fringe to each end of scarf as in photo.

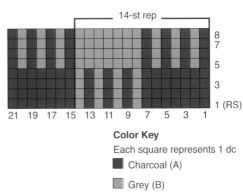

Color Key
Each square represents 1 dc
- ■ Charcoal (A)
- ■ Grey (B)

AQUA FRESH

Quenet

TOOLKIT

YARN

- (4) 5oz/140g, 450yd/410m of any worsted weight mohair blend in green (A) and blue (B)

HOOK

- Size I/9 (5.5mm) crochet hook or *size to obtain gauge*

FINISHED MEASUREMENTS

Approx 6½"/16.5cm wide x 64"/ 162.5cm long, excluding fringe

GAUGE

12 sts to 4"/10cm and 11 rows to 6"/15cm over pat st using 1 strand of A and B held tog and size I/9 (5.5mm) crochet hook.
Take time to check gauge.

STITCH GLOSSARY

Hdc2tog *Yo, insert hook into st, yo and pull up a lp (3 lps on hook); rep from * once more in same st, yo and through all 5 lps on hook, yo and draw lp through to finish.
Dc2tog Work 1 dc in next ch-1 sp until 2 lps rem on hook, work a 2nd dc into next ch-1 sp until 3 lps rem on hook, yo and through all 3 lps on hook.

PATTERN STITCH

Ch a multiple of 6 ch plus 2 extra.
Row 1 Work 1 sc in 2nd ch from hook, *ch 1, skip 2 ch, in next ch work (hdc2tog, ch 1) 3 times, skip 2 ch, 1 sc in next ch; rep from * to end, turn. **Row 2** Ch 4 (counts as 1 dc and ch 1), skip first ch-1 sp, 1 sc in next ch-1 sp, ch 3, 1 sc in next ch-1 sp, *ch 1, dc2tog over next 2 ch-1 sps, ch 1, 1 sc in next ch-1 sp, ch 3, 1 sc in next ch-1 sp; rep from * to last sc, skip last ch-1 sp, ch 1, 1 dc in last sc, turn. **Row 3** Ch 3 (counts as 1 hdc and ch 1), hdc2tog in first dc, ch 1, 1 sc in next ch-3 sp, ch 1, *in top of next dc2tog work (hdc2tog, ch 1) 3 times, 1 sc in next ch-3 sp, ch 1; rep from * to t-ch, in 3rd ch of ch-4 at beg of previous row work (hdc2tog, 1 hdc), turn. **Row 4** Ch 1, 1 sc in first hdc, 1 sc in first ch-1 sp, ch 1, dc2tog over next 2 ch-1 sp, ch 1, *1 sc in next ch-1 sp, ch 3, 1 sc in next ch-1 sp, ch 1, dc2tog over next 2 ch-1 sps, ch 1; rep from *, end 1 sc in 2nd ch of t-ch, turn. **Row 5** Ch 1, 1 sc in first sc, *ch 1, in top of next dc2tog work (hdc2tog, ch 1) 3 times, 1 sc in next ch-3 sp; rep from * end placing last sc in last sc, turn.
Rep rows 2-5 for pattern st.

SCARF

With 1 strand each A and B held tog, ch 20. Work in pat st until scarf measures 64"/62.5cm from beg.

FINISHING

Lightly block scarf.

FRINGE

Cut 11"/28cm length of yarn for each fringe. Alternate 3 strands of A for 1 fringe, 3 strands of B for 2nd fringe and 2 strands of A and 1 of B for third fringe and place 11 fringe along each end of scarf.

Quenet

TOOLKIT

YARN
- 🔢**1** 2²/₃oz/125g, 450yd/405m of any fingering weight wool

HOOK
- Size E/4 (3.5mm) crochet hook *or size to obtain gauge*

FINISHED MEASUREMENTS
Approx 6½"/16.5cm wide at lower edges and 48"/122cm long

GAUGE
12 sts and 16 rows to 2"/5cm over neck ribbing pat using size E/4 (3.5mm) hook. *Take time to check gauge.*

NOTE
The neck ribbing is worked lengthwise then each lace strip is worked downwards from the side (or row) edges of the neck ribbing.

SCARF
NECK RIBBING
Ch 80.
Row 1 Work 2 sc in 3rd ch from hook, work 1 sc in each rem ch to end. Ch 1, turn.
Row 2 Skip the first sc, insert hook into the back loop only of next st and work 1 sc through back lp (tbl), work 1 sc tbl in each sc to end, work 1 sc tbl in the t-ch. Ch 1, turn. Rep row 2 until there are 29 rows. Do not turn work after last rib row.

FIRST LACE STRIP
Set-up row Working along side of ribbed piece (into sides of rows), ch 3, 1 dc in next ridge, 1 dc in next ridge, *skip 1 furrow, ([work 1 dc, ch 1] 3 times, 1 dc) in next furrow*; rep between *'s to last 2 furrows, skip 1 furrow, 2 dc in last ridge—6 clusters made, turn.
Next row Ch 3, 1 dc in 2nd dc, *([work 1 dc, ch 1] 3 times, 1 dc) in middle of ch-1 sp of cluster; rep from *, end 2 dc in last sp. Rep this row until lace strip measures 15"/38cm. Join yarn to opposite edge of neck ribbing and work 2nd lace strip in same way.

FINISHING
Wash scarf in cool water. Do not wring or twist. Lay flat to block.

RIPPLE EFFECT

TOOLKIT

YARN

- (4) 10½oz/300g, 560yd/51-0m of any worsted weight mohair blend in denim blue (A)

- (4) 8¾oz/250g, 375yd/345m of any worsted weight ribbon yarn in lt blue (B)

HOOK

- Size J/10 (6mm) crochet hook or *size to obtain gauge*

FINISHED MEASUREMENTS

Approx 18"/46cm wide x 78"/198cm long

GAUGE

1 cluster pat and 6 pat rows to 3"/7.5cm.
Take time to check gauge.

STITCH GLOSSARY
WAVE STITCH PATTERN

Ch a multiple of 12 sts plus 6 extra.
Row 1 (RS) Work [1tr, ch 1] 3 times into 6th ch from hook, skip 5 ch, 1 sc in next ch, *ch 1, skip 5 ch, work [1 tr, ch 1] 7 times in next ch (for cluster), skip 5 ch, 1 sc in next ch; rep from * to last 6 ch, ch 1, work [1 tr, ch 1] 3 times in last ch, 1 tr in same ch as last 3 tr. Ch 1, turn.
Row 2 Work 1 sc in first tr, *ch 6, 1 sc in next sc, ch 6, skip 3 tr, 1 sc in next tr; rep from *, placing last sc into 4th ch of the ch 5 at beg of previous row. Ch 1, turn. **Row 3** Work 1 sc in first sc, *ch 6, 1 sc in next sc; rep from * to end. Ch 1, turn. **Row 4** Work 1 sc in first sc, *ch 1, work [1 tr, ch 1] 7 times in next sc, 1 sc in next sc; rep from * to end. Ch 1, turn. **Row 5** Work 1 sc in first sc, *ch 6, skip 3 tr, 1 sc in next tr, ch 6, 1 sc in next sc; rep from * to end. Ch 1, turn.
Row 6 Work 1 sc in first sc, *ch 6, 1 sc in next sc; rep from * to end. Ch 5, turn.
Row 7 Counting the ch 5 as 1 tr and ch 1, work [1 tr, ch 1] 3 times in first sc, 1 sc in next sc, *ch 1, work [1 tr, ch 1] 7 times in next sc, 1 sc in next sc; rep from* to last sc, work [ch 1, 1 tr] 4 times in last sc. Ch 1, turn.
Rep rows 2-7 for wave pattern st.

NOTES

1 When changing colors from A to B, draw the new color through last 2 loops on hook and ch and turn at end of row with the new color.
2 In order to avoid cutting and rejoining of yarns when it is necessary at color changes, fasten off the old color and leave at end of

Quenet

row, then return to the opposite end to pick up the new color and work row from this new starting position.

STOLE

With size J/10 (6mm) hook and A, ch 78.
Rows 1-4 Work pat rows 1-4 with A.
Rows 5 and 6 Work pat rows 5 and 6 with B.
***Row 7** Work pat row 7 with A.
Rows 8 and 9 Work pat rows 2 and 3 with B.
Row 10 Work pat row 4 with A.
Rows 11 and 12 Work pat rows 5 and 6 with B.* Rep between *'s (6-row pat rep) for color pat until piece measures approx 75"/ 190cm from beg, end with row 3 of wave pat st. Then with A only, work rows 4-7. Then with B, work row 2.
Last row Skip first sc, *work 1 sc in each of first 3 ch of ch-6 loop, ch 3, sl st in 3rd ch from hook (for picot), work 1 sc in each of next 3 ch of ch-6 loop, skip next sc; rep from * to end. Fasten off. Return to beg ch of stole and from RS, join B and work row 2 in beg ch sts across. With B, work last row as other end of stole. Fasten off.

FINISHING

Block stole from WS to measurements.

SPOKE MOTIF

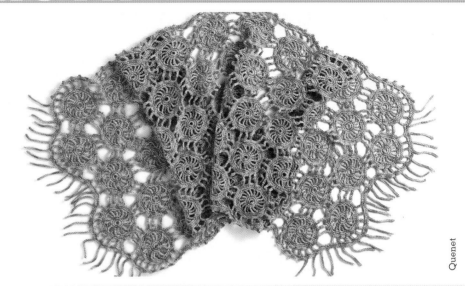

Quenet

TOOLKIT

YARN
- **2** 15¾oz/450g, 1230yd/1125m of any sport weight cotton

HOOK
- Size E/4 (3.5mm) crochet hook *or size to obtain gauge*

FINISHED MEASUREMENTS

Approx 20"/51cm wide x 68"/173cm long, excluding chain fringe

GAUGE

One spiral motif is 4½"/11.5cm across.
Take time to check gauge.

FIRST MOTIF

**Ch 6, join with sl st to first ch to form ring.
Rnd 1 Ch 1, 9 sc in ring. Join with sl st to first sc. **Rnd 2** Ch 1, 2 sc in each sc around. Join with sl st to first sc—18 sc. **Rnd 3** Ch 6 (counts as 1 tr and ch 2), skip first sc, [1 tr in next sc, ch 2] 17 times. Join with sl st to 4th ch of ch-6. **Rnd 4** Sl st in first ch-2 sp, ch 1, 2 sc in same sp as last sl st, *3 sc in next ch-2 sp, 2 sc in next ch-2 sp; rep from * to last ch-2 sp, 3 sc in last ch-2 sp. Join with sl st to first sc—45 sc. **Rnd 5** Ch 1, 1 sc in each of first 4 sc, *2 sc in next sc, 1 sc in each of next 4 sc; rep from * to last sc, 2 sc in last sc. Join with sl st to first sc—54 sc**. **Rnd 6 (picot round)** Ch 1, 1 sc in each of first 3 sc, *ch 4, sl st in 2nd and 3rd ch from hook, sl st in top of last sc (picot), 1 sc in each of next 3 sc; rep from * around, work picot over last sc. Join with sl st to first sc. Fasten off.

SECOND MOTIF

Rep from ** to ** on first motif.
Rnd 6 Ch 1, 1 sc in each of first 3 sc, ch 3, sl st in top of picot of adjoining motif, sl st in 2nd and 3rd ch from hook, sl st in top of last sc (for joining picot), [1 sc in each of next 3 sc, joining picot in next picot of adjoining motif] twice, *1 sc in each of next 3 sc, work ch-4 picot; rep from * to end of rnd, end ch-4 picot over last sc. Join with sl st to first sc. Fasten off. Make 65 motifs as for 2nd motif and join foll motif layout.

EDGING

Rnd 1 Beg at top right motif, join yarn with a sl st to first loose picot, [ch 4, sl st in top of next picot] 8 times, *ch 5, [sl st in top of next picot, ch 4] twice, sl st in next picot, [ch 5, sl st in next picot, (ch 4, sl st in top of next picot) 8 times]* twice, **ch 5, sl st in next picot, [ch 4, sl st in next picot] 5 times**; rep from ** to ** 10 times more, [ch 5, (sl st in next picot, ch 4) 8 times] twice, sl st in next picot; rep from * to * once, rep from ** to ** 11 times more, ch 5, [sl st in top of next picot, ch 4] 8 times, sl st in top of next picot, ch 5, join with sl st to first sc. **Rnd 2** Ch 1, [4 sc in next ch-4 sp] 8 times, *5 sc in next ch-5 sp, [4 sc in next ch-4 sp] twice, [5 sc in next ch-5 sp. (4 sc in next ch-4 sp) 8 times]* twice, **5 sc in next ch-5 sp, [4 sc in next ch-4 sp] 5 times**; rep from ** to ** 10 times more, 5 sc in next ch-5 sp, [4 sc in next ch-4 sp] 8 times; rep from * to * once, rep from ** to ** 11 times more, 5 sc in next ch-5 sp, [4 sc in next ch-4 sp] 8 times, 5 sc in next ch-5 sp, join with sl st to first sc.
Rnd 3 (fringe edging) Ch 1, 1 sc in same sp as last sl st, 1 sc in next sc, [ch 17, 1 sl st in 2nd ch from hook and in each ch to end of ch, sl st in top of last sc for 1 fringe, 1 sc in each of next 4 sc] 24 times, *[ch 3, sl st in top of last sc for small picot, 1 sc in each of next 4 sc] 81 times*, [work 1 fringe, 1 sc in each of next 4 sc] 28 times, rep from * to * once more, [work 1 fringe, 1 sc in each of next 4 sc] 3 times, work 1 fringe, 1 sc in each sc to end of rnd. Join with sl st to first sc. Fasten off.

Quenet

SCARF (side 1)

Beg at center with B, ch 322.

Row 1 (RS) Working into single (top) loop of foundation ch only, 1 sc in 2nd ch from hook, *1 sc in next ch, ch 1, skip 1 ch, 1 hdc in next ch, ch 1, skip 1 ch, 1 dc in next ch, [ch 1, skip 1 ch, 1 tr in next ch] twice, ch 1, skip 1 ch, 1 dc in next ch, ch 1, skip 1 ch, 1 hdc in next ch, ch 1, skip 1 ch, 1 sc in next ch, ch 1, skip 1 ch; rep from *, end last rep by working 2 sc in each of last 2 ch (do not skip 1 ch between the 2 sc), pull A through last 2 lps on hook, ch 1, turn. There are 321 sts and 20 wave pat reps.

Row 2 With A, 1 sc in each ch-sp and st across, ch 1, turn.

Row 3 With A, 1 sc in each sc across, drawing C through last 2 lps on hook, ch 1, turn.

Row 4 With C, ch 4 (counts as first tr), *1 tr in next st, ch 1, skip 1 st, 1 dc in next st, ch 1, skip 1 st, 1 hdc in next st, [ch 1, skip 1 st, 1 sc in next st] twice, ch 1, skip 1 st, 1 hdc in next st, ch 1, skip 1 st, 1 dc in next st, ch 1, skip 1 st, 1 tr in next st, ch 1, skip 1 st; rep from *, end last rep by working 2 tr in each of last 2 sts (do not skip 1 ch between the 2 tr), turn.

Row 5 Rep row 4.

Rows 6 and 7 Rep rows 2 and 3.

Rows 8 and 9 With B, ch 1, rep row 1, only working into sts instead of foundation ch, pull A through last 2 lps on hook, ch 1, turn.

Rows 10 and 11 Rep rows 2 and 3.

Rows 12 and 13 With D, rep rows 4 and 5, pull A through last 2 lps on hook, ch 1, turn.

Rows 14 and 15 Rep rows 2 and 3.

Fasten off.

SCARF (side 2)

With RS of piece facing and working along opposite side of foundation ch (into the unworked lps), work rows 1-15 as for side 1 with these color exceptions: for rows 4 and 5 use D instead of C and for rows 12 and 13 use C instead of D.

EDGING

For short edges of scarf, from RS join A with a sl st.

Row 1 (RS) Ch 1, work 39 sc evenly along end of scarf, ch 1, turn.

Row 2 Work 1 sc in each sc across. Fasten off.

TOOLKIT

YARN

- (3) 35oz/1000g, 1080yd/1000m of any DK weight cotton in white (A)

- 1¾oz/50g, 55yd/50m in yellow (B), green (C), and blue (D)

HOOK

- Size C/2 (2.75mm) crochet hook or *size to obtain gauge*

FINISHED MEASUREMENTS

Approx 7½"/19cm wide x 60"/152cm long

GAUGE

20 sc and 16 rows to 4"/10cm over sc pat st using size C/2 (2.75mm) hook.
Take time to check gauge.

NOTES

1 Work gauge swatch in sc only to determine proper gauge.

2 When working the wave pat rows in colors B, C and D, beg and end each row with either 2 sc or 2 tr.

3 Scarf is made lengthwise and from center to sides, first working side 1, then turning piece to work in opposite side of foundation row, side 2.

Quenet

TOOLKIT

YARN

- 2 1¾oz/50g, 175yd/160m of any sport weight wool in lilac (A), lime (B), lt green (C), med blue (D), pale green (E), pale blue (F), and lt blue (G)

HOOK

- Size D/3 (3mm) crochet hook *or size to obtain gauge*

FINISHED MEASUREMENTS

Approx 5½"/14cm wide x 50"/127cm long

GAUGE

28 sc and 28 rows to 4"/10cm over sc pat st using size D/3 (3mm) hook.
Take time to check gauge.

NOTES

1 The 7 colors are used in this design in a random combination of your choice. Just be sure that colors are alternated so that the same colors are not placed next to each other. 2 At completion of motifs, one more set of tails will be worked on 6 motifs to attach the discs and join the motifs to scarf points.

RECTANGLE MOTIF WITH TAIL (make 10 each of 6 colors, 9 of the 7th color for a total of 69)

Ch 14. **Row 1 (WS)** Work 1 hdc in 3rd ch from hook, 1 hdc in each ch to end—12 hdc. Ch 11 (for tail), turn. **Row 2** Work 1 sc in 2nd ch from hook, 1 sc in each of next 9 ch, 1 hdc in each of next 12 hdc, turn. **Row 3** Ch 2, 1 hdc in first 10 hdc, [yo and draw up a lp in next hdc] twice, yo and draw

through all 5 lps on hook for hdc2tog, turn, leaving rem sts unworked for tail. **Row 4** Ch 2, hdc2tog over first 2 sts, 1 hdc in next 7 hdc, hdc2tog over last 2 sts. Fasten off.

DISC (make 2 each of 6 colors for a total of 12)

Ch 2. **Rnd 1** Work 8 sc in 2nd ch from hook, join with sl st to first sc. Cont to work in rnds. **Rnd 2** Ch 1, work 2 sc in each sc around—16 sc. Join with sl st to first sc. **Rnd 3** Ch 1, 2 sc in first sc, *1 sc in next sc, 2 sc in next sc; rep from * to last sc, 1 sc in last sc—24 sc. Join with sl st to first sc. **Rnd 4** Ch 1, 1 sc in first sc, *2 sc in next sc, 1 sc in each of next 2 sc; rep from * to last 2 sc, 2 sc in next sc, 1 sc in last sc—32 sc. Join with sl st to first sc. **Rnd 5** Ch 1, 2 sc in first sc, *1 sc in each of next 3 sc, 2 sc in next sc; rep from * to last 3 sc, 1 sc in each of last 3 sc—40 sc. Join with sl st to first sc. Fasten off.

FINISHING

For 6 of the rectangle motifs, make one additional tail at opposite end of the rectangle as foll: join with sl st in matching color at center of rectangles, and ch 11, sc in 2nd ch from hook and in each ch. Fasten off. These 6 motifs with 2 tails will form one end of scarf. Then the end without the tails will be at center of the scarf. Foll photo, join motifs tog at points in the 6 alternating strips of [11 motifs, 12 motifs] 3 times. Join discs, alternating colors, to tail ends at each end of scarf.

TOOLKIT

YARN

- 3 5¼oz/150g, 415yd/375m of any DK weight cotton blend in lt teal (MC)

- 1¾oz/50g, 140yd/125m in dk teal (CC)

HOOK

- Size F/5 (3.75mm) crochet hook or *size to obtain gauge*

FINISHED MEASUREMENTS

Approx 4"/10cm wide x 70"/179cm long

GAUGES

4 ch-6 sps and 9 rows to 4"/10cm over trellis pat using size F/5 (3.75mm) crochet hook. One small flower is 3"/7.5cm across using size F/5 (3.75mm) crochet hook. One large flower is 4"/10cm across using size F/5 (3.75mm) crochet hook. *Take time to check gauges.*

NOTE

When changing colors from one rnd to the next, draw new color through sl st as you join the rnd.

STITCH GLOSSARY

Starting ring Make a slip knot 5"/12.5cm from tail end of yarn. Place slip knot on hook. To form starting ring, loosely wrap tail of yarn counter-clockwise around index finger of hand holding crochet hook. Slide ring off finger and work first round of sts into starting ring. After working the first round, pull gently on the yarn tail to close ring.
Long single crochet (Lsc) Insert hook into top of st of rnd below. Yo and draw up a lp that is the same height as working rnd. Yo and draw through both lps on hook to complete st.

SCARF

With MC, ch 22.
Row 1 Work (dc, ch 2, 2 dc) in 4th ch from hook, ch 2, sk next 2 ch, sc in next ch, *ch 6, sk next 3 ch, sc in next ch; rep from * twice more, ch 2, sk next 2 ch, work (2 dc, ch 2, 2 dc) in last ch (shell made). Ch 1, turn.
Row 2 Sk first dc, sl st in next dc and ch-2 sp, ch 3 (counts as 1 dc), work (dc, ch 2, 2 dc) in same ch-2 sp as sl st (beg shell made), ch 4, sk ch-2 sp, sc in next ch-6 sp, *ch 6, sc in next ch-6 sp; rep from * once more, ch 4, sk ch-2 sp, work shell in ch-2 sp of shell. Ch 1, turn.
Row 3 Sk first dc, sl st in next dc and ch-2 sp, ch 3 (counts as 1 dc), work beg shell in same ch-2 sp as sl st, ch 2, sc in next ch-4 sp, *ch 6, sc in next ch-sp; rep from * twice more, ch 2, work shell in last ch-2 sp. Ch 1, turn. Rep rows 2 and 3 for trellis pat until

piece measures 70"/179cm from beg (slightly stretched), end on row 3. Ch 1, turn.

TOP EDGING

Row 1 Sk first dc, sl st in next dc and ch-2 sp, ch 3, work beg shell in same ch-2 sp as sl st, sk ch-2 sp, tr in next sc, *work shell in next ch-6 sp, tr in next sc; rep from * twice more, work shell in ch-2 sp of last shell. Ch 3, turn.
Row 2 Work 6 dc in ch-2 sp of first shell, *sc in next tr, work 6 dc in ch-2 sp of next shell; rep from * 3 times more, ch 3, join ch with a sl st in 3rd ch of ch-3 t-ch of row below. Fasten off.

BOTTOM EDGING

Turn piece so RS is facing and bottom lps of foundation ch are at top. Join yarn with a sl st in bottom lp of first shell.
Row 1 Ch 3, work beg shell in same lp as joining, tr in bottom lp of next sc, *work shell in base of next ch-3 sp, tr in bottom lp of next sc; rep from * twice more, work shell in bottom lp of last shell. Ch 3, turn.
Row 2 Rep row 2 as for top edging. Fasten off.

SMALL BASIC FLOWER

MAKE STARTING RING

Rnd 1 (RS) Ch 1, work 8 sc in ring, join rnd with a sl st in first st—8 sts.

FIRST ROW OF PETALS

Rnd 2 Ch 1, sc in first st, *ch 3, sc in next sc; rep from * around 6 times more, end ch 3, join rnd with a sl st in first st—8 ch-3 sps.
Rnd 3 Ch 1, *work (sc, hdc, 2 dc, hdc, sc) in next ch-3 sp; rep from * around, join rnd with a sl st in first st—8 petals (48 sts). Fasten off.

SECOND ROW OF PETALS

Rnd 4 With RS facing, fold first row of petals towards you. Join yarn with a sl st between any 2 sts of rnd 3, ch 4, *sk next 4 sts, sc between next 2 sts, ch 4; rep from * around, join rnd with a sl st in beg sl st—12 ch-4 sps.
Rnd 5 Ch 1, work (sc, hdc, dc, 2 tr, dc, hdc, sc) in each ch-4 sp around, join rnd with a sl st in first st—12 petals. Fasten off.

FLOWER 1 (make 3 pieces)

Work rnds 1 and 2 using CC, rnds 3 and 4 using MC and rnd 5 using CC.

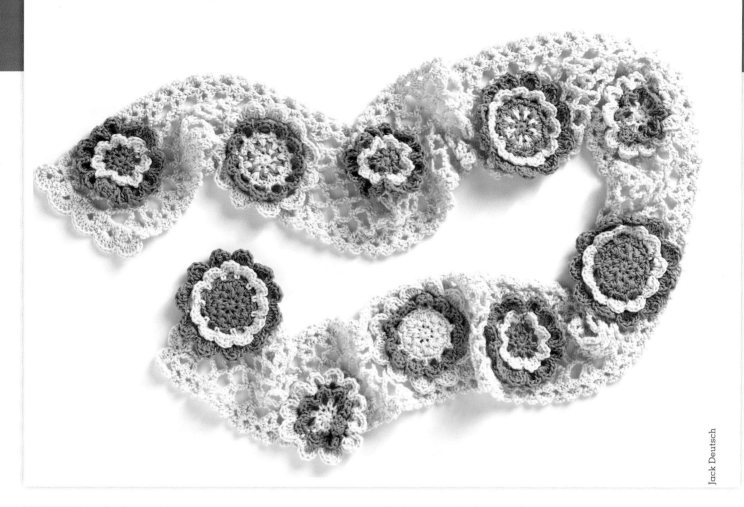

Jack Deutsch

FLOWER 2 (make 2 pieces)
Work rnds 1 and 2 using MC, rnds 3 and 4 using CC and rnd 5 using MC.

LARGE BASIC FLOWER

MAKE STARTING RING
Rnd 1 Ch 1, work 8 sc in ring, join rnd with a sl st in first st—8 sts.
Rnd 2 Ch 1, work 2 sc in each st around, join rnd with a sl st in first st—16 sts.
Rnd 3 Ch 1, work 2 sc in first st, Lsc over next st, [work 2 sc in next st, Lsc over next st] 7 times, join rnd with a sl st in first st—24 sts.
Rnd 4 Ch 1, work 2 Lsc over first st, sc in next 2 sts, [work 2 Lsc over next st, sc in next 2 sts] 7 times, join rnd with a sl st in first st—32 sts.

FIRST ROW OF PETALS
Rnd 5 Ch 3, sk first 2 sts, *sc in next st, sk next 2 sts, ch 3; rep from * around, join rnd with a sl st in first ch of beg ch-3—11 ch-3 sps.
Rnd 6 Ch 1, *work (sc, hdc, 2 dc, hdc, sc) in next ch-3 sp; rep from * around, join rnd with a sl st in first st—11 petals. Fasten off.

SECOND ROW OF PETALS
Rnd 7 With RS facing, fold first row of petals towards you. Join yarn with a sl st between any 2 dc of rnd 6, ch 4, *sc between 2 dc of next petal, ch 4; rep from * around, join with sl st in first sc—11 ch-3 sps.
Rnd 8 Ch 1, work (sc, hdc, dc, 2 tr, dc, hdc, sc) in each ch-4 lp around, join rnd with a sl st in first st—11 petals. Fasten off.

FLOWER 3
Work rnds 1-5 using CC, rnds 6 and 7 using MC and rnd 8 using CC.

FLOWER 4
Work rnds 1-4 using CC, rnds 5-7 using MC and rnd 8 using CC.

FLOWER 5
Work rnds 1-5 using MC, rnds 6 and 7 using CC and rnd 8 using MC.

FLOWER 6
Work rnds 1 and 2 using MC, rnd 3 using CC, rnds 4 and 5 using MC, rnds 6 and 7 using CC and rnd 8 using MC.

FLOWER 7
Work rnds 1 and 2 using CC, rnd 3 using MC, rnds 4 and 5 using CC, rnds 6 and 7 using MC and rnd 8 using CC.

FINISHING
Block scarf lightly to measurements. Referring to photo, arrange flowers on scarf, then sew in place.

Quenet

TOOLKIT

YARN
- (2) 3½oz/100g, 420yd/390m of any sport weight cotton

HOOK
Size C/2 (2.5mm) crochet hook or *size to obtain gauge*

FINISHED MEASUREMENTS
3½"/9cm wide x 42"/106.5cm long, excluding tassels

GAUGE
17 sts to 3"/7.5cm and 24 rows to 4"/10cm over sc pat st using size C/2 (2.5mm) hook. *Take time to check gauge.*

STITCH GLOSSARY
Fpdc (front post dc) Work from front to back around post of dc or fpdc into 2nd row below to make a dc post st and skip the sc behind this fpdc.

SCARF
Ch 21.

PREPARATION ROWS
Row 1 (RS) Sc in 2nd ch from hook and each of next 3 ch, [dc in each of next 4 ch, sc in each of next 4 ch] twice—20 sts. Ch 1, turn.
Row 2 Sc in each sc and dc across. Ch 1, turn.
Row 3 Sc in first 3 sc, *fpdc over next 2 dc, skip 2 sc behind fpdc, sc in next 2 sc; rep from * across, ending last rep sc in last 3 sc. Ch 1, turn.
Row 4 Sc in each sc and fpdc across—20 sts. Ch 1, turn.
Row 5 Sc in first 3 sc, *fpdc over next 2 fpdc, skip 2 sc behind fpdc, sc in next 2 sc; rep from * across, ending last rep sc in last 3 sc. Ch 1, turn.
Row 6 Rep row 4.

CABLE PANEL
Row 1 Sc in first 2 sc, [fpdc over fpdc] twice, skip 2 sc behind fpdc, sc in each of next 4 sc, fpdc over next 4 fpdc and skip 4 sc behind fpdc, sc in next 4 sc, [fpdc over fpdc] twice and skip 2 sc behind fpdcs, sc in last 2 sc. Ch 1, turn.
Row 2 and all WS rows Sc in each sc and fpdc across—20 sc. Ch 1, turn.
Row 3 Sc in first 2 sc, fpdc over 2 fpdc and skip 2 sc behind fpdc, sc in 4 sc, skip next 2 fpdc, fpdc over third and fourth fpdc, fpdc over first then second skipped fpdc—cable made, skip 4 sc behind fpdc, sc in 4 sc, fpdc over 2 fpdc, skip 2 sc behind fpdc, sc in last 2 sc. Ch 1, turn.
Row 5 Rep row 1.
Row 7 Rep row 1.
Row 9 Rep row 3.
Row 11 Sc in first 3 sc, *fpdc over next 2 fpdc, skip 2 sc behind fpdc, sc in next 2 sc; rep from * across, ending last rep sc in last 3 sc. Ch 1, turn.
Row 13 Sc in first 4 sc, [fpdc over next 4 fpdc, skip 4 sc behind fpdc, sc in next 4 sc] twice. Ch 1, turn.
Row 15 Sc in first 4 sc, [cable over next 4 fpdc, and skip 4 sc behind fpdc, sc in next 4 sc] twice. Ch 1, turn.
Row 17 Rep row 13.
Row 19 Rep row 13.
Row 21 Rep row 15.
Row 23 Rep row 11.
Row 24 Rep row 2.
Rep cable panel rows 1-24 for 7 times in total, then rep rows 1-13 once, rep row 2 and row 13. Fasten off.

BORDER (make 2)
With the RS facing, work 19 sc evenly along edge. Do not turn. Working from left to right, *ch 2, skip next sc, sc in next sc; rep from * across—9 ch-2 lps. Ch 2, turn.
Row 2 Skip first ch-2 lp, *sc in next ch-2 lp, ch 2; rep from * across, ending sc in last ch-2 lp. Ch 2, turn.
Rep row 2 until 2 ch-2 lps rem. Ch 2, turn.
Last row Skip first ch-2 lp, sl st in next ch-2 lp and fasten off.
Make two 3½"/9cm tassels and attach one to each ch-2 lp at points of border.

TOOLKIT

YARN
- (1) 5¼oz/150g, 570yd/525m of any fingering weight wool

HOOK
- Size E/4 (3.5mm) crochet hook *or size to obtain gauge*

FINISHED MEASUREMENTS
Approx 6"/15cm x 44"/112cm

GAUGE
6 popcorns and 13 rows to 4"/10cm over popcorn pattern stitch using size E/4 (3.5mm) hook. *Take time to check gauge.*

STITCH GLOSSARY
POPCORN STITCH PATTERN
Chain a multiple of 3 ch plus 2 extra ch.
Row 1 (RS) Work 1 sc in 2nd ch from hook, 1 sc in each ch to end. Ch 1, turn.
Row 2 (WS) Work 1 sc in first sc, *work 1 popcorn by (yo hook, draw up a lp) 5 times in next sc, yo and through all lps on hook, 1 sc in each of next 2 sc; rep from * to end. Ch 1, turn.
Row 3 Work 1 sc in each st to end. Ch 1, turn.
Row 4 *Work 1 sc in each of next 2 sc, work 1 popcorn in next sc; rep from *, end 1 sc in last sc. Ch 1, turn.
Row 5 Rep row 3.
Rep rows 2-5 for popcorn pattern stitch.

SCARF
Chain 29. Work popcorn pattern stitch on 9 popcorns until piece measures 44"/ 112cm from beg, end with pat row 2 or 4. Fasten off. Return to beg ch of scarf and working from WS, work pat row 4 into beg ch (this will give a matching popcorn edge at beg of scarf to look the same as end of scarf).

FINISHING
Block very lightly, if necessary, from WS.

Quenet

Jack Deutsch

TOOLKIT

YARN

- (4) 3½oz/100g, 310yd/285m of any worsted weight wool blend in purple (MC)

- (3) .88oz/25g, 230yd/210m of any DK weight mohair blend in olive green (A), burgundy (B), and gold (C)

HOOK

- Size G/6 (4mm) crochet hook or *size to obtain gauge*

FINISHED MEASUREMENTS

Approx 7"/17.5cm wide x 42"/106.5cm long (excluding fringe)

GAUGE

19 sts to 5"/12.5cm and 11 rows to 4"/10cm over dc pat st using size G/6 (4mm) crochet hook. *Take time to check gauge.*

SCARF

With MC, ch 165 loosely.
Row 1 (WS) Dc in 4th ch from hook and in each ch across—162 sts. Ch 3, turn.
Row 2 Working through back lps only, dc in each st across. Ch 3, turn.
Row 3 Working through front lps only, dc in each st across. Ch 3, turn. Rep rows 2 and 3 7 times more, then rep row 2 once—18 rows and 17 horizontal ridges of free lps. Fasten off.

FINISHING

Block scarf lightly to measurements.

TOP EDGING

With RS facing, join MC with a sl st in first st of row 18, ch 3, sl st in same st as joining, sl in next 3 sts, *ch 3, sl st in same st as last st, sl st in next 3 sts; rep from * across. Fasten off.

BOTTOM EDGING

With RS facing, join MC with a sl st in first bottom lp of foundation ch, ch 3, sl st in same lp as joining, sl in next 3 lps, *ch 3, sl st in same lp as last st, sl st in next 3 lps; rep from * across. Fasten off.

FRINGE AND SQUIGGLE EMBELLISHMENTS

For first fringe/squiggle, join MC with a sl st in right side edge of center horizontal ridge of free lps; ch 20 and fasten off. Rep on left side edge. Join C with a sl st in first ch at right edge.
Row 1 Ch 1, work 2 sc in same ch as joining, [work 2 sc in next ch] 19 times. Fold scarf along ridge of free lps, *work 2 sc in next free lp; rep from * to ch at left edge, [work 2 sc in next ch] 20 times. Ch 1, turn.
Row 2 Work 2 sc in each st across. Fasten off.
For second fringe/squiggle, skip 2 horizontal ridges up from first fringe/squiggle and join MC with a sl st in right side edge of next horizontal ridge; ch 20 and fasten off. Rep on left side edge. Cont to work as for first fringe/squiggle, using B.
For third fringe/squiggle, skip 2 horizontal ridges down from second fringe/squiggle and cont to work as for second fringe/squiggle, using A.
For fourth fringe/squiggle, skip 2 horizontal ridges up from second fringe/squiggle and join MC with a sl st in right side edge of next horizontal ridge; ch 20 and fasten off. Rep on left side edge. Cont to work as for first fringe/squiggle, using B.
For fifth fringe/squiggle, skip 2 horizontal ridges down from third fringe/ squiggle and cont to work as for fourth fringe/squiggle, using C.

POMPOMS (make 10 pieces)

With B, make 2 pompoms 1½"/4cm in diameter. Sew one to each end of first fringe. Make 4 pompoms using C and sew one to each end of second and third fringes. Make 4 pompoms using A and sew one to each end of fourth and fifth fringes.

TOOLKIT

YARN

- (4) 5¼oz/150g, 270yd/250m of any worsted weight cotton blend in burgundy (A)

- (5) 3½oz/100g, 240yd/220m of any bulky weight ribbon yarn in variegated pink (B)

HOOK

- Size E/4 (3.5mm) crochet hook or *size to obtain gauge*

Jack Deutsch

FINISHED MEASUREMENTS

Approx 4½"/11.5cm wide x 65"/165cm long (excluding fringe)

GAUGE

24 sts and 8 rows to 4"/10cm over base pat st using size E/4 (3.5mm) crochet hook. *Take time to check gauge.*

NOTE

The scarf is made in two steps: first make a base scarf using A and working from the bottom up. Then work a ribbon chain embellishment over the base scarf using B and working from the top down.

BASE SCARF

With A, ch 34.

Row 1 Dc in 8th ch from hook, sc in next ch, dc in next ch, *ch 3, sk 3 next ch, dc in next ch, sc in next ch, dc in next ch; rep from * across. Ch 5, turn.

Row 2 Work (dc, sc, dc) in first ch-sp, *ch 3, work (dc, sc, dc) in next ch-sp; rep from * across. Ch 5, turn. Rep row 2 for base pat st until piece measures 65"/165cm from beg. Fasten off.

RIBBON CHAIN EMBELLISHMENT

Join B with a sl st in last sc of last row of base scarf. Turn.

Row 1 *Ch 6, sl st in next sc; rep from * across. Ch 7, turn base scarf so last row worked is at bottom and the ch-7 is at right. Fold last row of ch-6 lps to back of work.

Row 2 Keeping yarn in front, insert hook into first ch-sp of base scarf and under ch-7 t-ch, yo and draw up a lp, then through lp on hook making a sl st, *ch 5, insert hook into next ch-sp of base scarf and under next B ch-lp and make sl st; rep from * across. Ch 7, turn. Rep row 2 for ribbon chain embellishment st to next to last row of base scarf. Ch 7, turn. To end, insert hook into first ch-sp of base scarf and under ch-7 t-ch and make a sl st. Fasten off.

FINISHING

Block scarf lightly to measurements.

FRINGE

Cut 20"/51cm strands of B. Using 4 strands for each fringe, attach 10 fringes evenly spaced across each end of scarf, knotting fringe around both the base scarf ch-lps and the B ch-lps. Tie ends evenly.

FLORAL MOTIF SCARF

TOOLKIT

YARN

- **2** 1¾oz/50g, 140yd/130m of any sport weight cotton in lt green (A), pink (B), yellow (C), lt pink (D) and coral (E)

HOOK

- Size F/5 (3.75mm) crochet hook or *size to obtain gauge*

FINISHED MEASUREMENTS

Approx 4½"/11.5cm wide x 48"/122cm long

GAUGES

One small flower is 1½"/4cm across using size F/5 (3.75mm) crochet hook.
One medium flower is 2¼"/5.5cm across using size F/5 (3.75mm) crochet hook.
One large flower is 2¾"/7cm across using size F/5 (3.75mm) crochet hook.
Take time to check gauges.

STITCH GLOSSARY

Cluster st (CL) [Yo and draw up a loop, yo and draw through 2 loops on hook] 3 times in next sp (or st), yo and draw though all loops on hook.

Long single crochet (Lsc) Insert hook into top of st of specified rnd below. Yo and draw up a lp that is the same height as working rnd. Yo and draw through both lps on hook to complete st.

SMALL BASIC FLOWER

With first color, ch 4. Join ch with a sl st forming a ring.
Rnd 1 Ch 1, work 12 sc in ring, join rnd with a sl st in first st. Fasten off.
Rnd 2 Join second color with a sl st in any sc, ch 1, sc in same sp as joining, *ch 2, CL in next sc, ch 2, sc in next sc; rep from * around, end CL in last sc, ch 2, join rnd with a sl st in first sc. Fasten off.

SMALL FLOWER 1 (make 9 pieces)
Use A for first color and B for second color.

SMALL FLOWER 2 (make 9 pieces)
Use C for first color and D for second color.

MEDIUM BASIC FLOWER

With first, ch 4. Join ch with a sl st forming a ring. **Rnd 1** Ch 1, work 9 sc in ring, join rnd with a sl st to first sc.

Rnd 2 Ch 1, work 2 sc in each sc around, join rnd with a sl st in first sc—18 sc. Fasten off.
Rnd 3 Join second color with a sl st in any sc, ch 1, sc in same sp as joining, *ch 3, sk next 2 sc, sc in next sc; rep from * around, end ch 3, sk last 2 sc, join rnd with a sl st in first sc.
Rnd 4 Ch 1, sc in same sp as joining, *ch 2, work 2 dc in next ch-3 sp, ch 2, sc in next sc; rep from * around, end ch 2, join rnd with a sl st in first sc. Fasten off.
Rnd 5 Join third color with a sl st in sp between any 2 dc, ch 1, sc in same sp as joining, *ch 3, Lsc in next sc of rnd 2, ch 3, sc in sp between next 2 dc; rep from * around, end ch 3, join rnd with a sl st in first sc. Fasten off.

MEDIUM FLOWER 1 (make 6 pieces)
Use A for first color, C for second color and E for third color.

MEDIUM FLOWER 2 (make 7 pieces)
Use C for first color, A for second color and B for third color.

LARGE BASIC FLOWER

With first color, ch 4. Join ch with a sl st forming a ring.
Rnd 1 Ch 4 (counts as dc and ch 1), [dc, ch 1] 7 times in ring, join rnd with a sl st in 3rd ch of beg ch-4. Fasten off.
Rnd 2 Join second color with a sl st in front lp of any dc, ch 1, sc in same sp as joining, *ch 2, work 2 dc in next ch-1 sp, ch 2, sc in front lp of next dc; rep from * around, end work 2 dc in last ch-1 sp, ch 2, join rnd with a sl st in first sc. Fasten off.
Rnd 3 Join third color with a sl st in free back lp of dc behind rnd 2, ch 1, sc in same lp as joining , *ch 4, sc in free back lp of next dc; rep from * around, end ch 4, join rnd with a sl st in first sc.
Rnd 4 Ch 1, sc in same sp as joining, *ch 2, work 4 dc in next ch-4 sp, ch 2, sc in next sc; rep from * around, end ch 2, join rnd with a sl st in first sc. Fasten off.

LARGE FLOWER 1 (make 7 pieces)
Use A for first color, D for second color and C for third color.

LARGE FLOWER 2 (make 6 pieces)
Use E for first color, C for second color and A for third color.

FINISHING

Arrange flowers on work surface in a 4½"/11.5cm wide x
48"/122cm long strip having 2 flowers side by side, but never
placing identical flowers together. Tack flowers together at
points where they touch using matching yarn color.

SPIKE STITCH SCARF

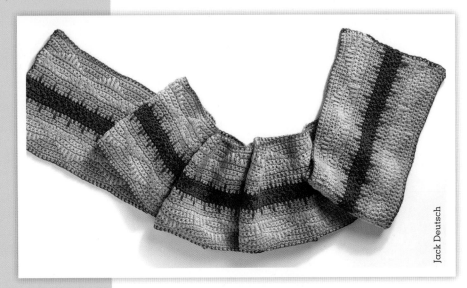

Jack Deutsch

TOOLKIT

YARN
- ![4] 10½oz/300g, 660yd/600m of any worsted weight wool in golden brown (A)
- 7oz/200g, 440yd/400m in pink (C)
- 3½oz/100g, 220yd/200m in seafoam green (B)

HOOK
- Size J/10 (6mm) crochet hook or *size to obtain gauge*

FINISHED MEASUREMENTS
Approx 9"/23cm wide x 97"/246.5cm long

GAUGE
12 sts and 20 rows to 4"/10cm over spike st using size J/10 (6mm) crochet hook.
Take time to check gauge.

NOTES
1 Scarf is made of 2 strips.
2 Strips are worked lengthways, then joined together.
3 When changing colors, draw new color through last 2 lps on hook, then ch and turn.

STITCH GLOSSARY
Spike stitch (SP st) Working from front to back, insert hook into top of st of specified rows below. Yo and draw up a lp that is the same height as working row. Yo and draw through both lps on hook to complete st.
SP2 Work SP st in top of st 2 rows below.
SP3 Work SP st in top of st 3 rows below.
SP4 Work SP st in top of st 4 rows below.
SP5 Work SP st in top of st 5 rows below.
SP6 Work SP st in top of st 6 rows below.

BLANKET STITCH

STRIP I
With A, ch 290.
Row 1 Sc in 2nd ch from hook and in each ch across—289 sts. Ch 1, turn.
Rows 2–5 Sc in each st across. Ch 1, turn.
Row 6 Rep row 2, changing to B in last st. Ch 1, turn.
Row 7 Sc in first 2 sts, *SP2 over next st, SP3 over next st, SP4 over next st, SP5 over next st, SP6 over next st, SP5 over next st, SP4 over next st, SP3 over next st, SP2 over next st, sc in next 3 sts; rep from * 23 times more, ending last rep with sc in last 2 sts. Ch 1, turn.
Rows 8–11 Rep row 2.
Row 12 Rep row 2, changing to A in last st. Ch 1, turn.
Row 13 Sc in first st, *SP6 over next st, SP5 over next st, SP4 over next st, SP3 over next st, SP2 over next st, sc in next st, SP2 over next st, SP3 over next st, SP4 over next st, SP5 over next st, SP6 over next st, sc in next st; rep from * across. Ch 1, turn.
Rows 14–17 Rep row 2.
Row 18 Rep row 2, changing to C in last st. Ch 1, turn.
Row 19 Sc in first st, *SP2 over next st, SP4 over next st, SP2 over next st, sc in next st; rep from * across. Ch 1, turn.
Rows 20 and 21 Rep row 2. Fasten off.

STRIP II
Work as for Strip I, but do not fasten off when row 21 is completed.

JOINING
Place strips tog so WS are facing and rows 21 are even.
Row 1 Ch 1, sl st in last st worked of Strip II, *sl st in corresponding st of Strip I, sl st in next st of Strip II; rep from *, end sl st in corresponding st of Strip I. Fasten off.

FINISHING
Block scarf lightly to measurements.

EMBROIDERY
With RS facing and C, embroider a row of blanket stitch (shown left) around entire edge.

FUN FAUX FUR

TOOLKIT

YARN
- (5) 7oz/200g, 350yd/320m of any bulky weight chenille yarn in lt green (A)

- (3) 5¼oz/150g, 360yd/330m of any DK weight wool in lt green (B)

HOOKS
- One each sizes I/9 (5.5mm) and J/10 (6mm) crochet hooks *or size to obtain gauge*

Quenet

FINISHED MEASUREMENTS
Approx 7½"/19cm x 74"/188cm, excluding chain trim

GAUGE
11 hdc to 4"/10cm and 2 hdc rows to 1¼"/3cm using A and size J/10 (6mm) hook. *Take time to check gauge.*

NOTE
Scarf is worked lengthwise. Be sure to chain loosely and to work pattern very loosely, especially when working with the lighter weight wool yarn.

SCARF
With size J/10 (6mm) hook and A, chain 200.
Row 1 (RS) With A, [yo and pull up a lp in 2nd ch from hook, yo and through 2 lps on hook] twice, yo and through all 3 lps for 1 puff st at the edge, work 1 hdc in each ch to last st, work 1 puff st in last st. Cut A. Rejoin A at beg to work next row from RS.
Row 2 (RS) Join A, ch 3, work 1 puff st in first st, work 1 hdc in each hdc to last st, work 1 puff st in last st, pulling B through last 2 lps on hook. Ch 1, turn.
Row 3 (WS) With B, working very loosely, work 1 sc in each hdc to end. Ch 1, turn.
Row 4 (RS) With B, working very loosely, work 1 sc in first sc, *ch 3, skip 3 sc, work 1 sc in next sc; rep from *, end 1 sc in last sc. Ch 1, turn.
Row 5 (WS) With B, working very loosely, work 1 sc in first 2 sc, *3 sc in ch-3 sp, 1 sc in next sc; rep from * to end, pulling A through last 2 lps on hook. Ch 3, turn.
Row 6 (RS) With A, work 1 puff st in first st, work 1 hdc in each st to last st, work 1 puff st in last st. Cut A. Rejoin A at beg to work next row from RS. Rep rows 2-6 three times more.
Next row (RS) *Work 1 hdc in each of next 7 hdc, yo and draw up a lp in next 2 sc, yo and through all lps on hook to dec 1 hdc; rep from * to last 2 hdc, 1 hdc in each of last 2 hdc, ch 1, turn.
Last row Work 1 sl st in each st across (to keep edge as firm as the beg chain edge). Fasten off.

FINISHING
Do not block or press.

CHAIN TAILS (make 10)
With size I/9 (5.5mm) hook and A, ch 3, join with sl st to first ch to form ring. **Rnd 1** Work 4 sc in ring. **Rnd 2** Work 1 sc in each sc around. Do not join. **Rnd 3** Rep rnd 2. **Rnd 4** *Pull up a lp in next 2 sc, yo and through 3 loops on hook; rep from * once.
Rnd 5 Rep from * of rnd 4 once, draw 2 strands B through last 2 loops on hook. With 2 strands B, ch 10. Pull through last lp of chain to attach to center of one strip in A. Fasten securely in place. Fasten all ends securely inside tail and to WS of scarf. Work all chain tails in same way.

Jack Deutsch

TOOLKIT

YARN

- (3) 7oz/200g, 440yd/400m of any DK weight wool

HOOK

- Size G/6 (4.5mm) crochet hook or *size to obtain gauge*

FINISHED MEASUREMENTS

Approx 4½"/11.5cm wide x 56"/142cm long (excluding fringe)

GAUGE

19 sts and 8 rows to 4"/10cm over cable pat using size G/6 (4mm) crochet hook. *Take time to check gauge.*

STITCH GLOSSARY

Front post treble crochet (FPtr) Yo twice, insert hook from front to back to front around post of specified st of row below, yo and draw up a lp, [yo and draw through 2 lps] three times.
Back post treble crochet (BPtr) Yo twice, insert hook from back to front to back around post (vertical bar) of specified st of row below, yo and draw up a lp, [yo and draw through 2 lps] three times.

SCARF

Ch 25.
Row 1 (WS) Dc in 4th ch from hook and in each ch across—22 dc. Ch 3, turn.

Row 2 Dc in first st, sk next 2 sts, FPtr around next 2 sts, FPtr around first sk st, then around 2nd sk st, FPtr around next 2 sts, *dc in next st, sk next 2 sts, FPtr around next 2 sts, FPtr around first sk st, then around 2nd sk st, FPtr around next 2 sts; rep from * once more, end dc in last st—three 6-st cables made. Ch 3, turn.
Row 3 Dc in first st, sk first 2 sts, BPtr around next 2 sts, BPtr around 2nd sk st, then 2d sk st, BPtr around next 2 sts, *dc in next dc, sk next 2 sts, BPtr around next 2 sts, BPtr in 2 skipped tr, BPtr in next 2 tr, rep from * once more, dc in last dc. Ch 3, turn. Rep rows 2 and 3 for cable pat until piece measures approx 56"/142cm from beg. Ch 3, turn.
Last row Dc in each st across. Fasten off.

FINISHING

Block scarf lightly to measurements.

FRINGE

Cut 10"/25.5cm strands of yarn. Using 10 strands for each fringe, attach 7 fringe evenly spaced across each end of scarf. Trim ends evenly.

COMING UP ROSES

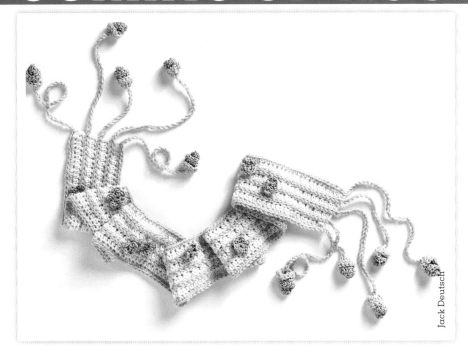

Jack Deutsch

TOOLKIT

YARN
- (3) 1¾oz/50g, 125yd/115m of any DK weight cotton blend in white (MC), lime (A), and pink (B)

HOOK
- Size G/6 (4mm) crochet hook or *size to obtain gauge*

FINISHED MEASUREMENTS
Approx 3"/7.5cm wide x 44"/111.5cm long (excluding fringe)

GAUGE
19 sts to 5"/12.5cm and 7 rows to 3"/ 7.5cm over hdc using size G/6 (4mm) crochet hook.
Take time to check gauge.

NOTES
1 Scarf is made lengthways.
2 When changing colors, draw new color through last 2 lps on hook.

SCARF
With MC, ch 169.
Foundation row (WS) Hdc in 3rd ch from hook and in each ch across—167 sts. Ch 2, turn.
Row 1 Hdc in first st, *ch 1, sk next st, hdc in next st; rep from * across. Ch 2, turn.
Row 2 Hdc in each st and ch-1 sp across. Ch 2, turn.
Rep rows 1 and 2 twice more. Fasten off.

FINISHING
Block scarf lightly to measurements.

FRINGE AND STRIPS
Each stripe is worked in chain st. Take care to maintain st gauge as you work. Position scarf so RS is facing and side edge (last row of scarf) is at top. For first fringe and stripe, with A, ch 30 for fringe. Insert hook into first ch-1 sp of row 1.
Row 1 Bring free end of yarn to WS of work, yo, draw through a lp and through lp on hook, *insert hook into next ch-1 sp, yo, draw through a lp and through lp on hook; rep from * across. Ch 20 for fringe. Fasten off. For 2nd fringe and stripe, with A, ch 14 for fringe. Insert hook into first ch-1 sp of row 3. Rep row 1 as for first fringe and stripe. Ch 28 for fringe. Fasten off. For 3rd fringe and stripe, with A, ch 24 for fringe. Insert hook into first ch-1 sp of row 5. Rep row 1 as for first fringe and stripe. Ch 13 for fringe. Fasten off.

SIDE FRINGE AND EDGING
Row 1 (RS) With A, ch 30 for fringe, sc in first st of last row of scarf, then sc each st across, ch 35 for fringe. Fasten off. Turn scarf so bottom edge is at top. **Row 1 (RS)** With A, ch 30 for fringe, sc between first and 2nd sts of foundation row, then sc between each st across, ch 35 for fringe. Fasten off.

LARGE ROSEBUDS
Join B with a sl st in end of first fringe at right. **Rnd 1** Ch 7, work 4 dc in 3rd ch from hook, work 4 dc in next 3 ch, sc in last ch, changing to A. **Rnd 2** Ch 3, work 10 dc in same ch as sc, join rnd with a sl st in 3rd ch of beg ch-3. Fasten off. Make a large rosebud in every other fringe at each end of scarf.

SMALL ROSEBUDS
Join B with a sl st in end of 2nd fringe at right. **Rnd 1** Ch 6, work 4 dc in 3rd ch from hook, work 4 dc in next 2 ch, sc in last ch, changing to A. **Rnd 2** Ch 3, work 8 dc in same ch as sc, join rnd with a sl st in 3rd ch of beg ch-3. Fasten off. Make a small rosebud in each rem fringe at each end of scarf.

FLOWERS (make 8 pieces)
With B, ch 4. Join ch with a sl st forming a ring. **Rnd 1** [Ch 4, sc in ring] 5 times. Fasten off. Arrange flowers as shown, then sew in place.

Quenet

FINISHED MEASUREMENTS

6½"/16.5cm wide x 66"/168cm long, excluding heart fringe

GAUGE

18 sts and 19 rows to 4"/10cm over stripe pat st using larger hook.
Take time to check gauge.

NOTES

1 Each sc and ch 1 is counted as 1 st.
2 When changing colors, work to last 2 loops of working color, draw new color through these last 2 loops and beg working with new color.

SCARF

With larger hook and A, loosely chain 298.
Row 1 (RS) Work 1 sc in 2nd ch from hook, *ch 1, skip 1 ch, 1 sc in next ch; rep from * to end, turn—297 sts. **Row 2** With A, ch 1, 1 sc in first sc, *1 sc in next ch-1 sp, ch 1, skip next sc; rep from * to last 2 sts, 1 sc in last ch-1 sp, 1 sc in last sc, joining B at end, turn. **Row 3** With B, ch 1, 1 sc in first sc, *ch 1, skip next sc, 1 sc in next ch-1 sp; rep from * to last 2 sts, ch 1, skip next st, 1 sc in last sc, turn. **Row 4** With B, rep row 2, joining A at end, turn. **Row 5** With A, rep row 3. **Row 6** With A, rep row 2.
Rep rows 3-6 for pat 6 times more. Fasten off.

HEART A (make 4)

With smaller hook and A, ch 2.
Rnd 1 Work 6 sc in 2nd ch from hook, join with sl st to first sc. **Rnd 2** Ch 1, 2 sc in each of the next 3 sc, 3 sc in next sc, 2 sc in each of the next 2 sc—13 sc. Do *not* join, turn. Work rem of heart in rows. **Row 3** Working around the first sc, work 1 dc in center sp of the first rnd, 1 sc in each of next 2 sc, 1 sl st in each of next 3 sc, 3 sc in next sc, 1 sl st in each of next 3 sc, 1 sc in each of next 2 sc; 1 dc around the last sc and into center sp of the first rnd, joining B at end, turn. **Row 4** With

B, ch 1, sc in first dc, 1 sc in each of next 2 sc, 1 sc in each of next 3 sl sts, 1 sc in next sc, 3 sc in next sc, 1 sc in next sc, 1 sc in next 3 sl sts, 1 sc in each of next 2 sc, 1 sc in last dc, 2 sc down side of same dc, sc3tog (by drawing up a lp in each of next 3 sc, yo, and through all loops on hook) over inner curve of heart, 2 sc up side of next dc, join with sl st to first sc. Fasten off.

HEART B (make 4)

Work as for heart A, substituting color A for B and B for A.

FINISHING

Alternating A and B hearts, sew hearts to scarf ends tacking through the 2 top corners of each heart and tacking hearts tog through one st at each side edge of heart (see photo).

FRINGE

Cut 14"/36cm lengths of A, having 6 lengths for each fringe. Pull fringe through each of the 3 heart points at both ends of scarf.

TOOLKIT

YARN

• ⓸ 7oz/200g, 450yd/410m of any worsted weight wool blend in black (A) and white (B)

HOOK

• One each size G/6(4.5mm) and I/9 (5.5mm) crochet hooks *or size to obtain gauge*

CORAL REEF

FINISHED MEASUREMENTS

Approx 9½"/24cm wide x 65"/165cm long

GAUGE

One motif is 5¼"/13.5cm across using size H/8 (5mm) crochet hook.
Take time to check gauge.

MOTIF A

Ch 4 (counts as 1 dc and 1 ch).
Rnd 1 (WS) Work 11 dc in 4th ch from hook, join rnd with a sl st in 3rd ch of beg ch-4—12 dc. Turn. **Rnd 2 (RS)** Ch 7 (counts as 1 dc and ch 4), *sk next st, dc in next st, ch 4; rep from * around, join rnd with a sl st in 3rd ch of beg ch-6—6 ch-4 sps. **Rnd 3** Sl st in first ch-sp, ch 3 (counts as 1 dc), work 4 dc in same ch-sp, *ch 4, work 5 dc into next ch-sp; rep from * 4 times more, to join rnd, ch 1, dc in 3rd ch of beg ch-3 (counts as 1 ch-4 sp)—6 ch-4 sps.
Rnd 4 Ch 3 (counts as 1 dc), work 2 dc in ch-sp created by dc, *ch 4, work (3 dc, ch 3, 3 dc) in next ch-sp; rep from * 4 times more, end ch 4, work 3 dc in beg ch-sp, to join rnd, dc in 3rd ch of beg ch-3 (counts as 1 ch-3 sp)—6 ch-3 sps and 6 ch-4 sps. **Rnd 5** *Ch 5, sl st in ch-4 sp, ch 5, sl st in next ch-3 sp; rep from * around, end ch 5, join rnd with a sl st in joining dc of rnd 4—12 ch-5 sps. Fasten off.

MOTIF B

Work as for motif A through rnd 4. **Joining Rnd 5** Ch 5, sl st in first ch-4 sp, ch 2, sl st in any ch-5 sp of motif A, ch 2, sl st into next ch-3 sp of motif B, ch 2, sl st in next ch-5 of motif A, ch 2, sl st in next ch-4 sp of motif B, cont to work motif B as foll: *ch 5, sl st in next ch-3 sp, ch 5, sl st in next ch-4 sp; rep from * around, end ch 5, join rnd with a sl st in joining dc of rnd 4—12 ch-5 sps. Fasten off.

MOTIF C

Work as for motif A through rnd 4. **Joining Rnd 5** Ch 5, sl st in first ch-4 sp, ch 2, sl st in ch-5 sp of motif B opposite joining of motifs A and B, ch 2, sl st in next ch-3 sp of motif C, ch 2, sl st in next ch-5 sp of motif B, ch 2, sl st in next ch-4 sp of motif C, cont to work motif C as foll: *ch 5, sl st in next ch-3 sp, ch 5, sl st in next ch-4 sp; rep from * around, end ch 5, join rnd with a sl st in joining dc of rnd 4—12 ch-5 sps. Fasten off. Referring to assembly diagram, cont to join 8 more motifs forming a strip of 11 motifs.

MOTIF D

Work as for motif A through rnd 4. **Joining Rnd 5**

Jack Deutsch

Ch 5, sl st in first ch-4 sp, ch 2, sk ch-5 sp before joining of motifs A and B, sl st in next ch-5 sp of motif A, ch 2, sl st in next ch-3 sp of motif D, ch 2, sl st in next ch-5 sp of motif A, ch 2, sl st in next ch-4 sp of motif D, ch 2, sl st in next ch-5 sp of motif B, ch 2, sl st in next ch-3 sp of motif D, ch 2, sl st in next ch-5 sp of motif B, ch 2, sl st in next ch-4 sp of motif D, cont to work motif D as foll: *ch 5, sl st in next ch-3 sp, ch 5, sl st in next ch-4 sp; rep from * around, end ch 5, join rnd with a sl st in joining dc of rnd 4—12 ch-5 sps. Fasten off.

MOTIF E

Work as for motif A through rnd 4. **Joining Rnd 5** Ch 5, sl st in first ch-4 sp, ch 2, sk ch-5 sp before joining of motifs C and D, sl st in next ch-5 sp of motif D, ch 2, sl st in next ch-3 sp of motif E, ch 2, sl st in next ch-5 sp of motif D, ch 2, sl st in next ch-4 sp of motif E, ch 2, sl st in next ch-5 sp of motif B, ch 2, sl st in next ch-3 sp of motif E, ch 2, sl st in next ch-5 sp of motif B, ch 2, sl st in next ch-4 sp of motif E, ch 2, sl st in next ch-5 sp of motif C, ch 2, sl st in next ch-3 sp of motif E, ch 2, sl st in next ch-5 sp of motif C, ch 2, sl st in next ch-4 sp of motif E, cont to work motif E as foll: *ch 5, sl st in next ch-3 sp, ch 5, sl st in next ch-4 sp; rep from * around, end ch 5, join rnd with a sl st in joining dc of rnd 4—12 ch-5 sps. Fasten off. Referring to assembly diagram, cont to join 8 more motifs to first strip of 11 motifs.

MOTIF F

Work as for motif A through rnd 4.
Joining Rnd 5 Work as for motif E, joining motif to last motif C and motif E only. Fasten off. Piece should measure approx 65"/165cm from beg.

FINISHING

Block scarf lightly to measurements.

TOOLKIT

YARN

- (4) 7oz/200g, 380yd/340m of any worsted weight cotton

HOOK

- Size H/8 (5mm) crochet hook or *size to obtain gauge*

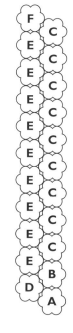

■■■□

FINISHED MEASUREMENTS
Approx 5"/12.5cm wide x 42"/106.5cm long

GAUGE
One doll is 3½"/9cm across and 4½"/11.5cm tall using size G/6 (4mm) crochet hook. *Take time to check gauge.*

BASIC DOLL IN DRESS
HEAD
With A, ch 3. Join ch with a sl st forming a ring. **Rnd 1** Ch 1, work 6 sc in ring, join rnd with a sl st in first sc. **Rnd 2** Ch 1, work 2 sc in each st around, join rnd with a sl st in first sc—12 sc. Ch 1, turn.

NECK
Row 1 Sc in first 2 sts. Ch 1, turn.
Row 2 Sc in each of 2 sts. Ch 10, turn.

FIRST ARM
Row 3 Hdc in 6th ch from hook, hdc in next 4 ch, sc in next 2 sts. Ch 10, turn.

SECOND ARM
Row 4 Hdc in 6th ch from hook, hdc in next 4 ch, join with a sl st in side edge of row 2. Fasten off.

HAIR
With RS of head facing, join 2nd color with a sl st in first st above right side edge of neck.
Row 1 Sc in same st as joining, [ch 5, sc in next sc] 9 times. Fasten off.

DRESS
Row 1 With 3rd color, ch 7 for right shoulder strap. Join ch with a sl st forming a ring. With RS of doll facing, slip ring onto doll's right arm. Sc in each of 2 center sts between arms, ch 7 for left shoulder strap, turn, wrap ch around left arm, join ch with a sl st in first ch forming a ring. Ch 1, turn.
Row 2 Work 2 sc in each sc—4 sc. Ch 1, turn.
Rows 3-9 Work 2 sc in first st, sc in each st across. Ch 1, turn.
Row 10 Sc in each of 11 sts. Fasten off.

DOLLS 1 AND 5
Use A for head, neck and arms. Use B for hair and dress.

DOLL 3
Use A for head, neck and arms. Use C for hair and B for dress.
DOLL 7
Use A for head, neck and arms. Use B for hair and C for dress.
DOLL 9
Use A for head, neck and arms. Use C for hair and dress.

BASIC DOLL IN OVERALLS
Work as for doll in dress until hair is completed.

OVERALLS
Rep rows 2 and 3 as for dress.
Row 3 Sc in each st across. Ch 1, turn.

FIRST LEG
Row 4 Sc in first 2 sts. Ch 1, turn.
Rows 5-8 Sc in each of 2 sts. Ch 1, turn.
Row 9 Rep row 5. Ch 5 for toe loop, turn.
Row 10 Rep row 5. Ch 1, turn to inside edge of leg, then sl st in each row to crotch. Fasten off.

SECOND LEG
Row 4 Join yarn with a sl st in next st after first leg, ch 1, sc in same st as joining, sc in last st. Ch 1, turn.
Rows 5-9 Sc in each of 2 sts. Ch 1, turn.
Row 10 Rep row 5. Ch 5 for toe loop, turn to inside edge of leg, then sl st in each row to crotch. Fasten off.

DOLL 2
Use A for head, neck and arms. Use C for hair and overalls.
DOLL 4
Use A for head, neck and arms. Use B for hair and C for overalls.
DOLL 6
Use A for head, neck and arms. Use C for hair and B for overalls.
DOLLS 8 AND 10
Use A for head, neck and arms. Use B for hair and overalls.

JOIN DOLLS WITH HEARTS
Working from right to left, place dolls 1 through 10 on work surface.
Row 1 (RS) With D, make a slip knot. Place dolls 1 and 2 with WS tog. Insert hook through t-ch of right arm of doll 1 and t-ch of

TOOLKIT

YARN
- (4) 4½oz/125g, 250yd/230m of any worsted weight cotton in yellow (A), cobalt blue (B), kelly green (C), and scarlet (D)

HOOK
- Size G/6 (4mm) crochet hook or *size to obtain gauge*

left arm of doll 2. Place slip knot on hook. Draw lp of slip knot through, yo and draw through lp, then sc in same sp as joining. Ch 1, turn.

Row 2 Work 2 sc in sc. Ch 1, turn.

Row 3 Work 2 sc in each st—4 sc. Ch 1, turn.

Row 4 Work 2 sc in first st, sc in next 2 sts, work 2 sc in last st, join with a sl st in 2nd hair loop of doll 2—6 sc. Ch 1, turn.

Row 5 Work 2 sc in first st, sc in next 4 sts, work 2 sc in last st, join with a sl st in 2nd hair loop of doll 1—8 sc. Ch 1, turn.

Row 6 Sk first st, work 5 dc in next st, sk next st, sl st in next st, sk next st, work 5 dc in next st, sk next st, sl st in last st. Fasten off. Working in this manner, cont to join doll 2 to doll 3, doll 3 to doll 4, etc.

FINISHING

Block scarf lightly to measurements.

EDGINGS

Grass

Turn scarf so RS is facing and bottom edge is at top. Join C with a sl st in t-ch of right arm of doll 10. **Row 1** Ch 9, sc in ch-5 toe loop of doll, *sc in next 2 ch of toe loop, sc in next 2 sc of leg, ch 3, sc in next 2 sc of next leg, sc in next 2 ch of next toe loop, ch 3, sc in next 11 sts of next doll, ch 3; rep from * across, ch 9, join with a sl st in t-ch of left arm of doll 1. Ch 2, turn.

Row 2 Work 12 hdc in first ch-9 sp, hdc in each sc and ch to opposite ch-9 sp, end work 12 hdc in 2nd ch-9 sp, drawing B through all 3 lps on hook to complete last hdc.

Sky

Row 1 Ch 3, dc in 2nd hair loop of doll 1, ch 9, *sc in 5th hair loop, ch 7, sc in 3rd dc of first shoulder of heart, ch 5, sc in 2nd shoulder of heart, ch 7; rep* across, end ch 9, dc in 2nd hair loop of doll 10, ch 4, join with a sl st in first C hdc. Ch 1, turn. **Row 2** Work 5 sc in first ch-4 sp, sc in next dc, work 11 hdc in next ch-9 sp, *hdc in next sc, work 7 hdc in next ch-7 sp, hdc in next sc, work 5 hdc in next ch-5 sp, hdc in next sc, work 7 hdc in next ch-7 sp; rep from * across, end hdc in last sc, work 11 hdc in last ch-9 sp, sc in last dc, work 5 sc in last ch-4 sp. Fasten off.

HEART TRIM

Center heart

With RS facing, locate 2 center sts on short end of scarf. Join D with a sl st in first of these 2 sts. **Row 1** Sc in same st as joining, sc in next st. Ch 1, turn. **Row 2** Sc in each of 2

Jack Deutsch

sts. Ch 1, turn. **Row 3** Work 2 sc in each st—4 sc. Ch 1, turn. **Row 4** Work 2 sc in first st, sc in next 2 sts, work 2 sc in last st—6 sc. Ch 1, turn. **Row 5** Work 2 sc in first st, sc in next 4 sts, work 2 sc in last st—8 sc. Turn. **Row 6** Sk first st, work 5 dc in next st, sk next st, sl st in next st, sk next st, work 5 dc in next st, sk next st, sl st in last st. Fasten off.

Second heart

With RS facing, sk 6 sts to the right of center heart. Join D with a sl st in the 7th st. Rep rows 1-5 as for center heart. Turn. **Row 6** Sl st in first dc of shoulder of center heart, sk first st of second heart, work 5 dc in next st, sk next st, sl st in next st, sk next st, work 5 dc in next st, sk next st, sl st in last st. Fasten off.

Third heart

With RS facing, sk 5 sts to the left of center heart. Join D with a sl st in next st. Cont to work as for second heart to row 6. **Row 6** Sk first st, work 5 dc in next st, sk next st, sl st in next st, sk next st, work 5 dc in next st, sk next st, sl st in last st, then sl st in first dc of shoulder of center heart. Fasten off. Rep heart trim at opposite end of scarf.

Quenet

TOOLKIT

YARN

- (4) .88oz/25g, 110yd/100m of any worsted weight mohair blend in light green (A), green (B) and brown (C)

HOOK

- Size I/9 (5.5mm) crochet hook *or size to obtain gauge*

FINISHED MEASUREMENTS

Approx 5"/12.5cm wide x 65"/165cm long (excluding fringe)

GAUGE

One 9-dc scallop to 2¾"/7cm and 6 rows to 2½"/6.5cm over scallop pat st using size I/9 (5.5mm) crochet hook.
Take time to check gauge.

STITCH GLOSSARY

SCALLOP STITCH PATTERN

Chain a multiple of 11 ch plus 10.

Row 1 Work 1 dc in 4th ch from hook, ch 1, skip 2 ch, 1 sc in next ch, *ch 5, skip 4 ch, 1 sc in next ch, ch 1, skip 2 ch, work (1 dc, ch 1, 1 dc) in next ch, ch 1, skip 2 ch, 1 sc in next ch; rep from *, end ch 2, skip 2 ch, 1 dc in last ch. Ch 1, turn.
Row 2 Work 1 sc in first dc, skip ch-2 sp, *work 3 dc in next each of next 3 ch 1-sps, 1 sc in next ch-5 sp; rep from *, end 3 dc in last ch-1 sp, 2 dc in 3rd ch of t-ch. Ch 4, turn.
Row 3 Work 1 sc in between 2nd and 3rd dc, *ch 1, in next sc work (1 dc, ch 1, 1 dc), ch 1, 1 sc in between next 3rd and 4th dc, ch 5, 1 sc in between next 3rd and 4th dc; rep from *, end ch 1, 2 dc in last sc, skip t-ch. Ch 3, turn.
Row 4 Work 1 dc in first dc, 3 dc in ch-1 sp, *1 sc in ch-5 sp, work 3 dc in each of next 3 ch-1 sps; rep from *, end 1 sc in t-ch sp. Ch 3, turn.
Row 5 Work 1 dc in first sc, ch 1, *1 sc in between next 3rd and 4th dc, ch 5, 1 sc in between next 3rd and 4th dc, ch 1, work (1 dc, ch 1, 1 dc) in next sc, ch 1; rep from *, end 1 sc in between 3rd and 4th dc, ch 2, 1 dc in 3rd ch of t-ch. Ch 1, turn.
Rep rows 2-5 for scallop pattern st.

SCARF

With A, ch 263.
Note Leave a 6"/15cm length of each color when cutting and beg with a new color.
With A, work rows 1 and 2 of pat st. With B, work rows 3 and 4 of pat st. With C, work rows 5 and 2 of pat st. With B, work rows 3 and 4 of pat st. With A, work rows 5 and 2 of pat st. With C, work rows 3 and 4 of pat st. Fasten off.

FINISHING

Block scarf lightly to measurements.

FRINGE

Cut 16 strands 11"/28cm long of each A, B and C. Fold each fringe in half and pull through where 6"/15cm length ends of scarf were left. Trim ends evenly.